THE REALLY, REA[LLY]

HORRIBLE

KIDS'

JOKE

BOOK

THE REALLY, REALLY HORRIBLE KIDS' JOKE BOOK

KAREN KING AND PATIENCE COSTER

ARCTURUS

ARCTURUS

This edition published in 2013 by Arcturus Publishing Limited
26/27 Bickels Yard, 151–153 Bermondsey Street,
London SE1 3HA

Designed by Elaine Wilkinson
All images from Shutterstock.

ISBN: 978-1-78212-326-2
CH003642EN

Supplier 05, Date 0713, Print Run 2540

Printed in Singapore

CONTENTS

WANT TO GROSS OUT (AND OUTGROSS!) YOUR FRIENDS? WANT TO TICKLE THEIR FUNNY BONES AT THE SAME TIME?

Then this bumper collection of jokes about weird animals and peculiar people (INCLUDING ZOMBIES) is for you!

Impress your teachers with your grasp of **HORRIBLE HISTORY** and **SMELLY SCIENCE**! Disgust your parents with **YUCKY ONE-LINERS**! Dive into the pond of green **SLIMY GLOOP** that is . . .

THE REALLY, REALLY HORRIBLE KIDS' JOKE BOOK!

What did the skunk say when the wind changed?
It's all coming back to me now.

How many skunks does it take to make a big stink?
A phew!

Why aren't elephants allowed on the beach?
Their trunks might fall down.

What do you get if you cross a Tyrannosaurus and a skunk?
A stinkosaurus.

There was a lady from Niger
Who went for a ride on a tiger.
Not long after that,
The tiger got fat
With the lady from Niger
inside her.

How do elephants play squash?
They jump on one another.

Why do ostriches have such long legs?
So they can't smell their feet.

Why do gorillas have big nostrils?
Have you seen the size of their fingers?!

What do you call a man who keeps a wild ferret down his pants?
Stupid!

What is a polygon?
A dead parrot.

What's wet, smelly and goes ba-bump, ba-bump?
A skunk in a tumble drier.

What's brown and dangerous and lives in a tree?
A monkey with a machine gun.

Why are skunks always arguing?
Because they like to raise a stink.

What do you call a bloodsucking bat that attacks pigs?
A hampire.

What do you call a flying skunk?
A smellicopter.

What do you get if you cross an elephant with a ton of prunes?
Out of the way.

Why did the porcupine cross the road?
To show that he had guts.

How many arms does an alligator have?
It depends on how much of its dinner it's eaten!

What do you give a sick bird?
Tweetment.

What's the difference between a coyote and a flea?
One howls on the prairie, and the other prowls on the hairy.

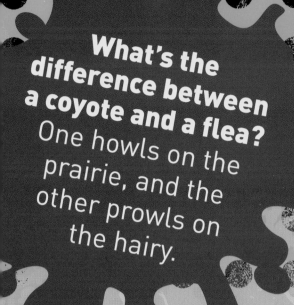

What do you call an exploding monkey?
A baboom!

Did you hear about the frog who had his legs chopped off?
He was very un-hoppy.

What did the lion say when he saw the kid on a skateboard?
Meals on wheels!

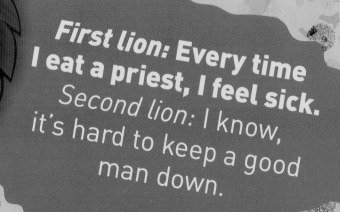

First lion: Every time I eat a priest, I feel sick.
Second lion: I know, it's hard to keep a good man down.

Hickory, Dickory Dock,
Two mice ran up the clock.
The clock struck one,
But the other managed
to get away.

Why was the young kangaroo thrown out by his mother?
For jumping on the bed.

Where do sparrows get their glasses from?
Bird's Eye.

What did they call the canary that flew into the pastry dish?
Tweetie Pie.

What do you get if you cross an elephant with a kangaroo?
Holes all over Australia.

Knock, knock!
Who's there?
Panther.
Panther who?
Panther what you wear on your legs.

How do you stop a fish from smelling?
Cut off its nose.

What do you call a large African mammal with a runny nose?
A rhi-snot-erous.

How do porcupines play leapfrog?
Very carefully.

What's green and gross and lives under the sea?
Shark snort!

Knock, knock!
Who's there?
Lionel.
Lionel who?
Lionel roar if you step on its tail.

Knock, knock!
Who's there?
Ash.
Ash who?
Ash-ark who just ate your family and now I'm going to eat you!

What do sharks like to eat?
Kid fingers and chips.

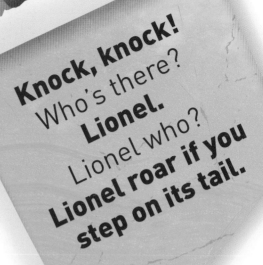

Waiter! Bring me a crocodile sandwich immediately!
I'll make it snappy, sir!

There was a young lady from Crewe
Who found a dead mouse in her stew,
Said the waiter: "Don't shout and wave it about,
Or the others will all want one, too!"

What do sharks call human children?
Appetizers.

Waiter, Waiter! There are feathers in my custard!
That's right, sir, it's Bird's custard.

What's green, has four legs, and a tail?
A seasick rat.

What do you get if you cross a bear with a cowpat?
Winnie the Pooh.

What did the evil chicken lay? Devilled eggs.

What do you get if you cross a chicken with a skunk? A fowl smell.

Why did the dirty chicken cross the road? For some fowl purpose!

What's black and white and green and brown? A cow with a runny nose in a muddy field.

Waiter, waiter! This chicken has dots on it. It's OK, sir, it's only chicken pox.

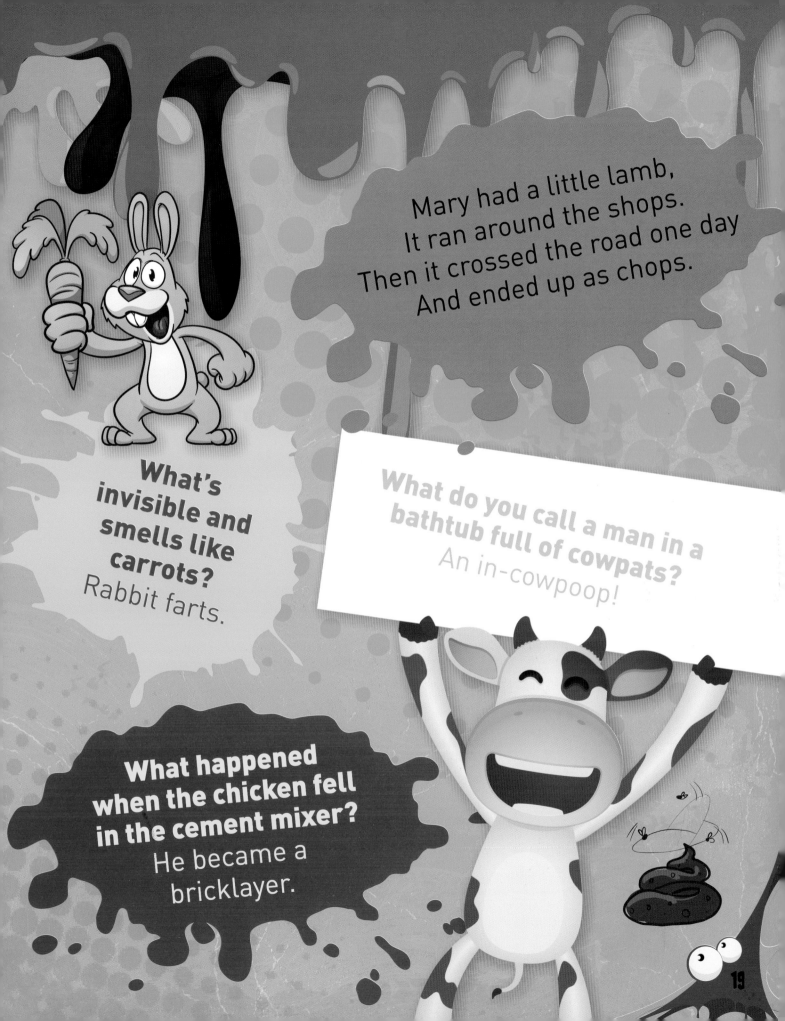

Mary had a little lamb,
It ran around the shops.
Then it crossed the road one day
And ended up as chops.

What's invisible and smells like carrots?
Rabbit farts.

What do you call a man in a bathtub full of cowpats?
An in-cowpoop!

What happened when the chicken fell in the cement mixer?
He became a bricklayer.

What has fangs and webbed feet?
Count Duckula.

What happened when the cow jumped over the barbed wire fence?
She had an udder catastrophe.

What goes Ooooo! Oooooo!
A cow with no lips!

Where do you find a chicken with no legs?
Exactly where you left it.

What do you get if you sit under a cow?
A pat on the head.

What do you get if you cross King Kong with a budgie?
A messy cage.

Mary had a little lamb,
It rolled around in poo.
And everywhere that Mary went,
Her smelly lamb went, too.

What do you call
a sheep with
a machine gun?
Lambo.

Why did half a
chicken cross
the road?
To get to his
other side.

Don't ever kiss your bunny,
When its nose is runny,
It will taste all funny,
Because you'll get a lot
Of green, yukky snot!

Goosey, Goosey, Gander
Where does he wander?
In and out the farmyard
Looking for a snack,
Saw a little mouse
And gobbled it up.
Now the goose goes squeak
Instead of going quack.

Why do mice need oiling?
Because they squeak.

What do you call a cow with no legs?
Ground beef.

Why is a turkey like an evil little creature?
Because it's always a-goblin.

What do you get from naughty cows?
Bad milk.

23

How do you know that owls are smarter than chickens? Have you ever heard of Kentucky Fried Owl?

Knock, knock!
Who's there?
Goose.
Goose who?
Goose who's knocking at your door!

What did the black cat do when its tail was cut off? It went to a re-tail store.

What's worse than a bull in a china shop? A porcupine in a balloon factory.

Two cows were talking in the field.
1st cow: Are you worried about this mad cow disease?
2nd cow: Why should I be? I'm a penguin.

Why is a kitten like an unhealed wound?
Both are a little puss-y.

Little sausage dog
Crossing the street
Here comes a speeding car
Now it's sausage meat!

My dog saw a sign saying Wet Paint.
So he did.

What do you get if you cross a cat with a canary?
A full tummy.

What do cats like for breakfast?
Mice Krispies.

There was once a large tabby cat
Who swallowed a whole cricket bat.
He swallowed the ball,
The wickets and all,
So the cricket team clobbered him flat.

What kind of market do dogs avoid?
Flea markets.

Tim: **This loaf of bread is nice and warm.**
Sarah: It should be, the cat's been sitting on it all day!

!!!

What's the difference between a maggot and a cockroach?
Cockroaches crunch more when you eat them.

Which animals didn't go to the ark in pairs?
Maggots. They went in apples!

How do you keep flies out of the kitchen?
Put a bucket of manure in the hallway.

What's another word for a python?
A mega-bite.

Why didn't the viper viper nose?
Because the adder adder hankie.

What do worms leave around the top of bathtubs?
The scum of the earth.

What did one maggot say to the other maggot?
What's a nice girl like you doing in a joint like this?

What's the maggot army called?
The apple corps.

What do you get if you cross a bee with a skunk?
A creature that stinks and stings.

What's yellow and goes round and round at 60 miles an hour?
A mouldy frog in a blender.

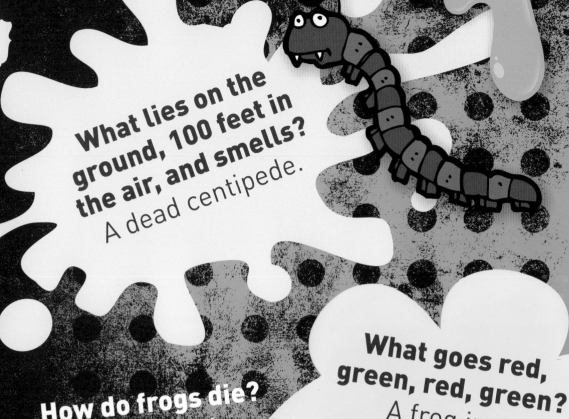

What lies on the ground, 100 feet in the air, and smells?
A dead centipede.

How do frogs die?
They Kermit suicide.

What goes red, green, red, green?
A frog in a blender.

What did the slug say as he slid down the wall?
How slime flies!

What happened when a daddy longlegs crawled into the salad?
It became a daddy shortlegs.

What's white on the outside and green in the middle?
A frog sandwich.

What are the most faithful insects on the planet?
Fleas. Once they find someone they like, they won't leave.

What did the fisherman use as a bookmark?
A flatfish to mark his plaice.

Knock, knock!
Who's there?
Woodworm.
Woodworm who?
Woodworm cake be enough, or would you like two?

What's the difference between school lunches and a pile of slugs?
School lunches come on a plate.

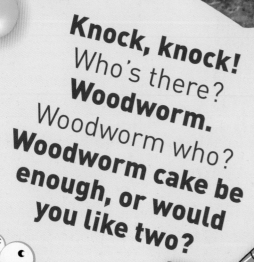

Knock Knock!
Who's there?
Thumping.
Thumping who?
Thumping green and slimy ith climbing up your back!

Little Miss Muffet
Sat on a tuffet
Eating a bowl of stew.
Along came a spider
And sat down beside her,
So she ate that up, too.

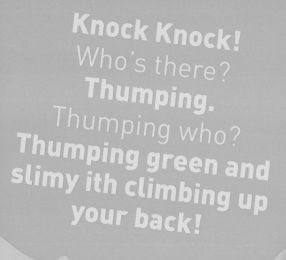

Waiter, waiter! What's wrong with this fish?
Long time no sea, sir!

Knock, knock!
Who's there?
Snake.
Snake who?
Quick! Snake a run for it!

33

Knock, knock!
Who's there?
Maggot.
Maggot who?
Maggot me this new dress today.

Knock, knock!
Who's there?
Moth.
Moth who?
Moth get myself a key.

What's yellow, wriggly, and dangerous?
A maggot with attitude.

What hand would you use to grab a poisonous snake?
Your enemy's.

What did the snake say to the cornered rat?
Hiss is the end of the line, pal!

Knock, knock!
Who's there?
Viper.
Viper who?
Viper your nose!

What's the difference between a worm and an apple?
Have you tried eating worm pie?

What's wet and slippery and likes Latin American music?
A conga eel.

What do you get when you cross a flea with a rabbit?
Bugs Bunny.

What's green and slimy and found at the North Pole?
A lost frog.

Why did the maggot cross the road?
To get to the dead chicken.

Waiter, waiter! There's a slug in my salad.
I'm sorry, sir, I didn't know you were a vegetarian.

I wish I was a little grub
With whiskers round my tummy.
I'd climb into a honey pot
And make my tummy gummy.

Where do tadpoles change?
In the croakroom.

Waiter, waiter! I can't eat this meat, it's crawling with maggots.
Quick, run to the end of the table, you can catch it as it goes by!

What's the difference between bogies and broccoli?
Kids don't eat broccoli.

What has a bottom at the top?
Legs.

Did you hear the joke about the toilet?
I can't tell you, it's too dirty!

What does a headless horseman ride?
A nightmare.

There was a young lady from Surrey
Who made a big pot of curry
She ate the whole lot
Straight from the pot
And had to dash to the loo in a hurry.

A belch is a gust of wind
That cometh from the heart,
But should it take a downward trend
It turneth to a fart.

Why did the man
with one hand
cross the road?
To get to the
secondhand
shop.

There was a young woman
named Emma,
Who was seized with
a terrible tremor.
She swallowed a spider,
Which wriggled inside her
And left Emma in
a dilemma.

What did one
toilet say to
the other?
You look
flushed.

Knock, knock!
Who's there?
Tom Sawyer.
Tom Sawyer who?
Tom Sawyer butt when you were changing your pants!

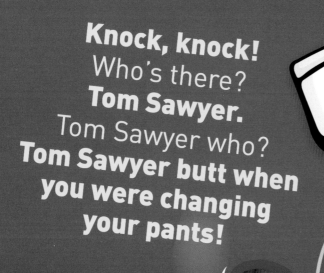

What do you do if your nose goes on strike?
Picket.

Why did the nose cross the road?
Because it was tired of getting picked on.

What did one eye say to the other?
Between you and me, something smells.

Laugh and the world laughs with you.
Fart and you stand alone.

What do you call a tramp with short legs?
A low-down bum.

Knock, knock!
Who's there?
Anita.
Anita who?
Anita go to the bathroom.

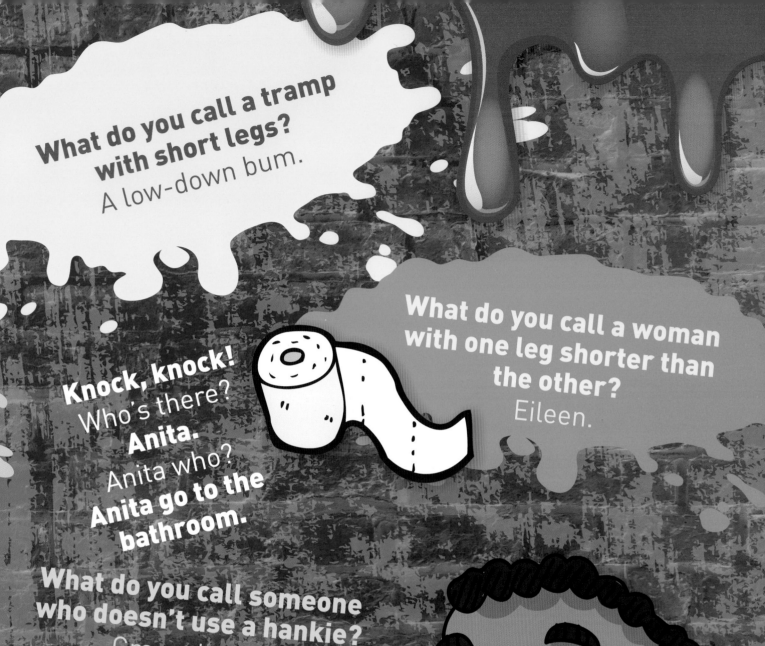

What do you call a woman with one leg shorter than the other?
Eileen.

What do you call someone who doesn't use a hankie?
Greensleeves.

What do you call someone who never blows his nose?
Ronnie.

There was an old man from Peru
Who dreamed he was eating his shoe.
He awoke in the night
In a terrible fright
And found it was perfectly true.

What do you call a man with a bus on his head?
Dead.

Which two letters are bad for your teeth?
DK

Knock, knock!
Who's there?
Dan.
Dan who?
Dandruff.

When are broken bones useful?
When they start to knit.

Why was the nose sad? Because it didn't get picked.

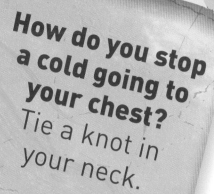

How do you stop a cold going to your chest? Tie a knot in your neck.

When are eyes not eyes? When the wind makes them water.

What should you take if you're run down? The number of the car that hit you.

What goes ha ha boing? A man laughing his head off.

HA, HA!

Why was the nose tired?
Because it kept running.

Teacher: Did you pick your nose?
Johnny: No, I was born with it.

What did one tonsil say to the other tonsil?
Get dressed, the doctor is taking us out tonight!

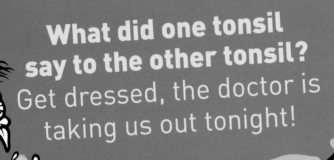

What colour is a belch?
Burple.

How many knees do people have?
Four. Your left knee, your right knee, and your two kid-nees!

What is the perfect cure for dandruff?
Baldness.

What's red and stupid?
A blood clot.

Amy: My brother's in the hospital.
Ella: What's wrong with him?
Amy: He has spotted fever.
Ella: Is it dangerous?
Amy: No, it was spotted just in time.

What goes boo, hoo, splat?
Someone crying their eyes out.

What do you do if you split your sides laughing?
Run until you get a stitch.

Did you hear the joke about the body snatchers?
I'd better not tell you, you might get carried away.

Why did the man put corn in his shoes?
Because he had pigeon toes.

Why did the secretary cut off her fingers?
She wanted to write shorthand.

Did you hear about the cross-eyed teacher?
He couldn't control his pupils.

There was a young man named Art
Who thought he'd be terribly smart.
He ate tons of beans
And busted his jeans
With a loud and earth-shattering fart.

Why did the farmer have sore feet?
A tractor ran over his corn.

How do you define agony?
A one-armed man with an itchy butt hanging from a cliff top.

What do you get if you cross a burglar with a cement mixer?
A hardened criminal.

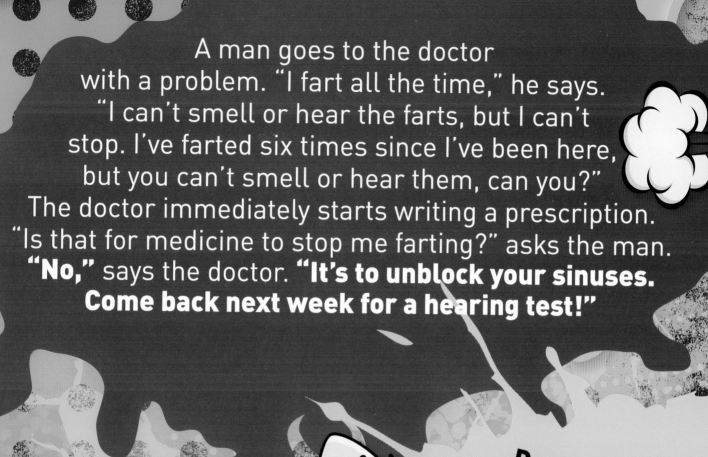

A man goes to the doctor with a problem. "I fart all the time," he says. "I can't smell or hear the farts, but I can't stop. I've farted six times since I've been here, but you can't smell or hear them, can you?" The doctor immediately starts writing a prescription. "Is that for medicine to stop me farting?" asks the man. **"No,"** says the doctor. **"It's to unblock your sinuses. Come back next week for a hearing test!"**

What do you do if you swallow a spoon? Just sit there quietly and don't stir.

Doctor, doctor, I've got athlete's foot in my head. What makes you think that? **My nose keeps running.**

Patient: Doctor, I'm having trouble getting to sleep. Doctor: Lie on the edge of the bed and you'll soon drop off!

49

What happened when the idiot had a brain transplant?
The brain rejected him.

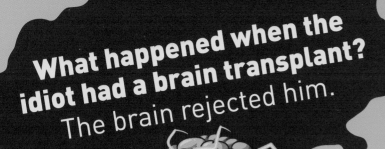

What do you do if your kidneys are bad?
Take them back to the butcher.

Doctor, doctor, my head is splitting.
Let me axe you one or two questions.

Surgeon: I'm sorry, sir, but I left a sponge inside you when I operated last week.
Patient: So that's why I keep feeling thirsty.

Doctor, I've got double vision. What can I do?
Go around with one eye closed.

Doctor, doctor, I've broken my arm in **two places.** Well, don't go back there again.

Doctor: **Why did you eat a pencil sharpener?** Patient: I was trying to sharpen my appetite.

Did you hear about the plastic surgeon? He sat in front of the fireplace and melted.

Doctor, can you give me something for wind? Yes, here's a kite.

Doctor, doctor, I've got a terribly sore throat. Go to the window and stick your tongue out. **Will that cure it?** No, I just don't like the woman who lives opposite.

Doctor, I keep getting a pain in my eye when I drink coffee.
Try taking the spoon out of the cup.

Doctor, doctor, I don't like all these flies buzzing around my head.
Point out the ones you do like and I'll swat the rest.

Doctor, I'm having trouble breathing.
I'll give you something that will soon put a stop to that!

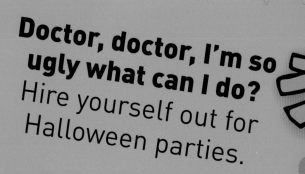

Doctor, doctor, I'm so ugly what can I do?
Hire yourself out for Halloween parties.

Doctor, doctor, I keep thinking I'm a caterpillar. Don't worry, you'll soon change.

Jack: Have you seen the new doctor? He'll have you in stitches! Lily: I hope not. I've only come for a checkup!

Will this ointment clear my pimples, doctor? I never make rash promises.

What kind of bandage do people wear after heart surgery? Ticker tape.

A woman comes into the doctor's office with two little children who are crying. **"Why is your son crying?"** asks the doctor. "Because he has four peas stuck up his nose," explains the woman. **"And why is the little girl crying?"** "Because she wants the rest of her lunch back!"

Mother: Doctor, my son's just swallowed some gunpowder.
Doctor: Well, don't point him at me!

Surgeon to patient: I'm sorry to tell you that we've amputated the wrong leg. But don't worry, the man in the next bed wants to buy your shoes!

Patient: I'm really worried about my son's nail-biting habit.
Doctor: Don't worry, nail-biting is very common in children.
Patient: What, six-inch rusty ones?

Worried patient: Tell me the truth, doctor, is it serious?
Doctor: Well, I wouldn't start watching a new TV series if I were you.

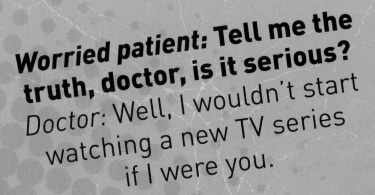

What do little zombies play?
Corpses and robbers.

What do you use to flatten a ghost?
A spirit level.

What did the zombie get his medal for?
Deadication.

Knock, knock!
Who's there?
Zombie.
Zombie who?
Zombies make honey, some bees are queens.

How do you know when a zombie is tired?
He's dead on his feet.

What do ghosts do on their holidays?
Fright-water rafting.

What rooms don't zombies like?
Living rooms.

What streets do ghosts haunt?
Dead ends.

What do you call a brainy monster?
Frank Einstein.

Knock, knock!
Who's there?
Havana.
Havana who?
**Havana a spooky
old time!**

**What do
ghosts like to
play at a party?**
Hide-and-shriek.

**What are pupils
at ghost school
called?**
Ghoulboys and
ghoulgirls.

**Who did the ghost
invite to his party?**
Anyone he could dig up.

58

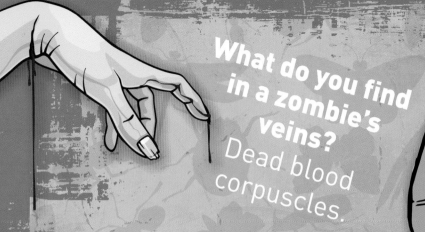

What do you find in a zombie's veins? Dead blood corpuscles.

Did you hear what the zombie's friend said when he saw his new girlfriend? Good grief! Where did you dig her up from?

First ghoul: Am I late for dinner? Second ghoul: Yes, everyone's been eaten.

Who looks after a haunted house? Skeleton staff.

Knock, knock! Who's there? **Turner** Turner who? **Turner round very slowly, there's a zombie behind you!**

Where do you go to buy a zombie?
To the Mon-Store.

Why do ghosts like strawberries for pudding?
Because they come with scream.

Knock, knock!
Who's there?
Coffin.
Coffin who?
Coffin and splutterin'.

Where do zombies go on cruises?
The Deaditerranean.

What does Dracula say to his victims?
It's been nice gnawing you.

Why is Hollywood full of vampires?
They need someone to play the bit parts.

What do you call an overweight vampire?
Draculard.

What do vampires play poker for?
High stakes.

How do you catch a vampire fish?
With bloodworms.

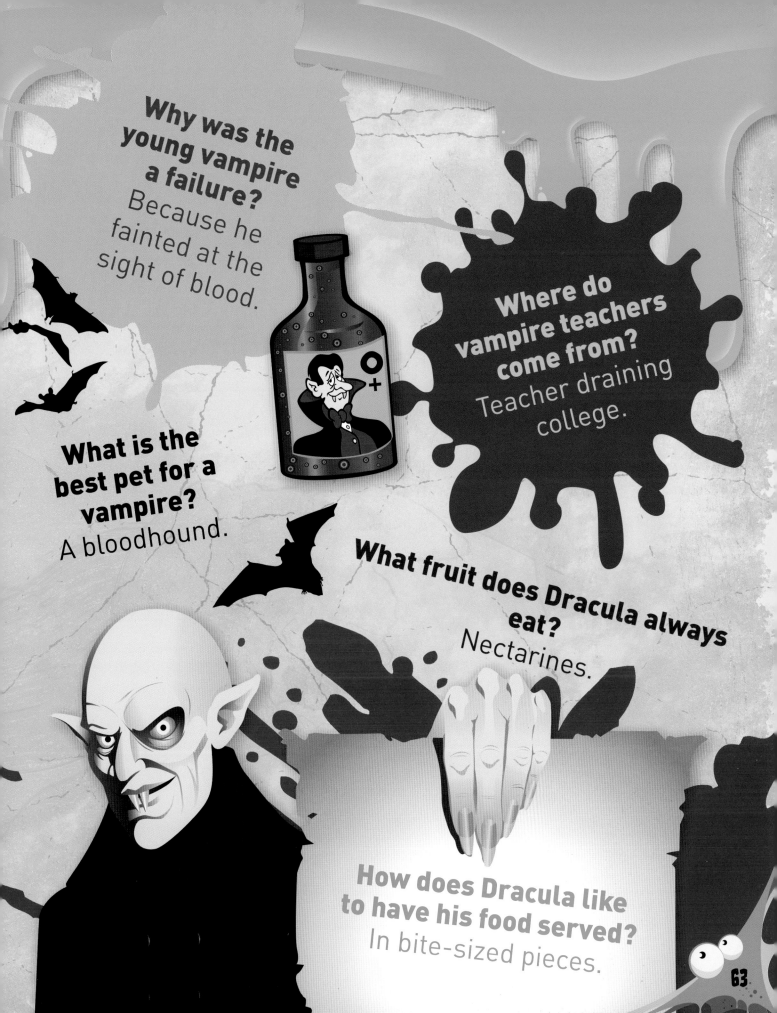

Why was the young vampire a failure? Because he fainted at the sight of blood.

Where do vampire teachers come from? Teacher draining college.

What is the best pet for a vampire? A bloodhound.

What fruit does Dracula always eat? Nectarines.

How does Dracula like to have his food served? In bite-sized pieces.

Why wouldn't the vampire postman deliver the letter?
He was on his coffin break.

What game do cannibals love to play?
Swallow my leader.

What do you get if you cross a vampire with a flea?
Lots of very worried dogs.

Did you hear about the vampire who was locked up in an asylum?
He was batty.

What is the U.S national holiday for vampires?
Fangsgiving Day.

What did the cannibal chef make of his new kitchen assistant?
Burgers!

Why was the cannibal expelled from school?
Because he kept buttering up the teachers.

What hangs around at night and goes chomp, suck, ouch!?
A vampire with fangache.

Why do vampires never get fat?
They eat necks to nothing.

A cannibal from Penzance
Ate an uncle and two aunts,
A cow and a calf,
An ox and a half,
And now he bursts out of
his pants.

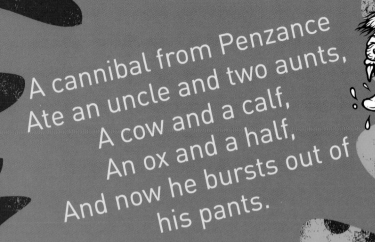

Two cannibals are tucking into a big pot of soup.
First cannibal: Your wife makes delicious soup. *Second cannibal:* **Yes, but I'll miss her.**

Two cannibals are tucking into a clown.
First cannibal: Does this taste a bit funny to you?

What kind of beans do cannibals like best? Human beans.

What does a caveman give his wife on Valentine's Day?
Ugs and kisses.

What do you call a caveman who's been buried since the Stone Age?
Peat.

What are Ancient Egyptian parents called?
Mummies and deadies.

What does a T. rex call a snack?
A caveman.

A mummy next to the Nile
Hadn't been out in a while,
So she strolled into town
In a long evening gown,
And everyone there
ran a mile.

Why did the Romans build straight roads?
So their soldiers didn't go around the bend.

What do the Greek gods drink with their breakfast?
Orange Zeus.

How was the Roman Empire cut in half?
With a pair of Caesars.

What do you get when you cross a mummy with a vampire bat?
A flying band-aid.

Why did the Roman Colosseum have to close?
The lions had eaten up all the prophets!

What do you get in a five-star pyramid?
A tomb with a view.

Which Roman emperor is the windiest?
A-gust-us.

What do you get if you cross a mummy with a car mechanic?
A toot and car man.

How do mummies hide?
They wear masking tape.

Why did the minotaur keep knocking over pots?
He was like a bull in a china shop!

Why did the Romans build straight roads in Ancient Britain?
So the Britons couldn't lie in ambush around the corner.

What do you call armoured pyjamas?
Knight nighties.

What can you say about the terrible mummy joke?
It sphinx.

Did you hear about the angry mummy? He flipped his lid.

Where do mummies go for a swim? To the Dead Sea.

A Roman emperor asked his soothsayer to tell him the future. "I'm afraid your wife is going to die very suddenly," said the soothsayer. Two days later, the emperor's wife died. The emperor was very angry and ordered the soothsayer to come to him immediately. "Let's see if you can tell me when **you** are going to die," said the emperor. Terrified, the soothsayer replied: "I don't know when I am going to die, but I do know that you will die two days later!"

What ancient civilization was the hardest to clean up?
Mess-Opotamia.

Did you hear about the Roman running for election in the Senate?
He took a stab at it.

Why did the mummy call the doctor?
Because it was coffin.

73

What is a prehistoric monster called when it's asleep?
A dinosnore.

What game did the Ancient Greeks play?
Hydra and seek.

What do you call a Roman emperor with a cold?
Julius Sneezer.

Why are Ancient Egyptian children confused?
Because their daddies are mummies.

What do you call a friendly pharoah?
A chummy mummy.

How fast can a caveman run?
It depends on the size of the dinosaur chasing him!

What does the 1286BC inscribed on the Ancient Egyptian's tomb indicate?
The registration of the chariot that ran him over!

Why do mummies make excellent spies?
They're good at keeping things under wraps.

How do we know Moses wore a wig?
Because sometimes he was seen with Aaron and sometimes without.

Why do Stone Age people eat sloths all the time?
Because they believe fast food is bad for you.

Why do mummies seldom take holidays?
They don't want to relax and unwind.

How does the Roman cannibal feel about his mother-in-law?
Gladiator.

What did the people of Minos pave their roads with?
Mino-tar.

77

GHASTLY CHARACTERS

Why did Blackbeard wear headphones?
He liked listening to pirate radio.

Why did the court jester swallow fire?
Because he wanted to burn some calories!

How did Columbus's men sleep on their ships?
With their eyes shut.

Why did the cowboy die with his boots on?
Because he didn't want to stub his toes when he kicked the bucket.

Why was George Washington buried at Mount Vernon?
Because he was dead.

What do you get when you cross a U.S. president with a shark?
Jaws Washington.

Why did everyone agree with the awesome swordsman?
He knew how to drive home a good point.

Who conquered half the world, laying eggs along the way?
Attila the Hen.

How much did the pirate pay for his peg leg and hook?
An arm and a leg.

What did the pirate cry as he fell overboard?
Water way to go!

Why do archers shoot arrows?
Could it be they are trying to get a point across?

An ancestor of mine came over on the **Mayflower.** Really? Which rat was he?

Abraham Lincoln's assassin had a table in a diner named after him. They called it the John Wilkes Booth.

A pirate with an eye patch, a hook, and a peg leg walks into a tavern. The bartender says, "You look like you've been in lots of sea battles. How did you get the peg leg?" The pirate answers, "Arr, a cannonball blew me leg right off!" "Wow!" says the bartender, "And how about the hook?" "Arr, me hand was eaten by a shark on the high seas!" "That's amazing! And the eye patch?" "Arr, a seagull pooped in me eye." Confused, the bartender asks, "How can you lose your eye from seagull poop?" "Well, it was me first day with the hook."

What is the moral of the story of Jonah and the whale?
You can't keep a good man down.

Which protest by a group of cats and dogs took place in 1773?
The Boston Flea Party.

Why don't pirates do the dishes before they walk the plank?
Because they wash up on shore later.

There was a bold
pirate of Boulder,
Whose cutlass was slung
from his shoulder.
He'd mighty fine notions
Of plundering oceans,
But his dad said: "Perhaps,
when you're older."

What did the executioner say to the prisoner? Time to head off.

What do you get if a famous French general steps on a landmine? Napoleon Blownapart.

How did the Hunchback of Notre Dame cure his sore throat? He gargoyled.

A tired, hungry medieval peasant arrives at a roadside inn with a sign reading "George and the Dragon". He knocks on the door. The innkeeper's wife sticks her head out of the window. "Please can you spare some food?" the man asks. "No!" the woman shouts. "Could I have a drink of water?" "No!" she growls. "Could I at least use your bathroom?" "No!" she roars again. "Do you suppose," the man says, "I could speak to George?"

Did you hear about the schoolgirl who was studying mythical monsters? When her teacher asked her to name something half-man and half-beast, she said: "Buffalo Bill".

Who is the biggest gangster in the sea? Al Caprawn.

Did prehistoric people hunt bear? No, they wore clothes!

What do you call a highwayman who is ill? Sick Turpin.

What do you call a pirate with four eyes? A piiiirate.

What's yellow, tasty and conquered most of Europe and Asia?
Genghis Khan on the cob.

What do you get if you cross a vampire with Al Capone?
A fangster.

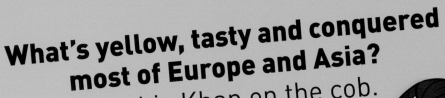

Why did the witchfinder spend so long at the beach?
He was looking for a sandwich.

The executioner told his assistant to hold the basket in front of the chopping block.
"If we don't do this right," he said, "heads will roll."

First medieval prisoner: How come you're so tall?
Second medieval prisoner: I was sentenced to a long stretch.

What happened when the gladiator put his head into a lion's mouth to count how many teeth the lion had? The lion closed its mouth to see how many heads the gladiator had.

After the great battle on the border between France and Germany, where did they bury the survivors? You don't bury survivors, silly!

Friar Tuck was a monk, so why did he get involved in a life of crime? It was his habit.

A three-legged dog walks into a saloon in the Old West. He hobbles up to the bar and says: "I'm looking for the man who shot my paw."

Why do dragons breathe fire?
Because they don't like raw meat.

What happens when the Queen burps?
She gets a royal pardon.

How was King Henry VIII different from normal husbands?
He married his wives first and axed them afterwards.

Why didn't Henry VIII's marriages last?
At least two of his wives found him a pain in the neck.

What did the dragon say when he saw St George in his shining armour?
Oh no, not more tinned food.

What did the ghost of Queen Elizabeth I say as it floated through the terrified woman's bedroom?
Don't worry, I'm just passing through.

Lady: **We had boar for dinner last night.**
Knight: Wild?
Lady: **Let's just say he wasn't too happy.**

Which queen belched the most?
Queen Hic-toria.

In medieval England, it was the custom for the heir to the throne to wear a fancy collar known as a ruff. One heir wore a very fancy ruff, known as a dandy ruff. It blocked his vision and meant he kept tripping over. This proves that dandy ruffs cause falling heirs.

Why did Henry VIII have so many wives?
He liked to chop and change.

Why do dragons have such sharp teeth?
Because the knights are always in cans.

Which queen was the fattest?
Mary, Queen of Scones.

Why did Henry VIII need an oxygen tank?
Because he couldn't breathe with no heir.

Where did Anastasia go?
I don't know. She must have been Romanov.

Why did the knight pull out of the archery contest?
He found it an arrowing experience.

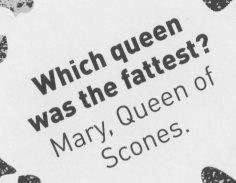

Why do dragons sleep all day?
So they can fight knights.

In days of old
When knights were bold,
Before toilets were invented,
They left their load
Along the road
And walked away contented.

How do you get ahead in life?
Become a royal executioner.

What do you call a tiny man in a tin suit?
A mite in shining armour.

Why was the ghost of Anne Boleyn always running after the ghost of Henry VIII?
She was trying to get a-head.

Three knights came across a dragon in the forest. The dragon said, "I'm going to eat you." The first knight said, "Wait! Let's make a deal. Let each of us tell you something we think you can't do. If you can do it, you may eat us." The dragon agreed to the deal. Said the first knight: "Go to the barn and eat 16 rooms full of hay." The dragon did it. Said the second knight: "Drink half the water in the ocean." The dragon did this. The third knight burped and said: "Catch it and paint it green."

In days of old
When men were bold,
And pants were made of tin,
No mortal cry
Escaped a guy
Who sat down on a pin.

Teacher:
If William Braveheart Wallace was alive today, he would be looked on as a remarkable man.
Student: Yes, he'd be more than 600 years old!

Why did some kings like uprisings?
They found them a peasant surprise.

Scotsman:
Did you hear the joke about the museum in Scotland that had a skull of Mary Queen of Scots when she was 12 in one room and a skull of Mary Queen of Scots when she was 30 in another?
Englishman: No, what was it?

What do you get hanging from the walls of an Elizabethan castle?
Tired arms.

When did Queen Elizabeth I die?
A few days before they buried her.

A knight returns to the king's castle with prisoners and bags of gold. "Tell me of your adventures," says the king. "Well, sire, for weeks I have robbed and stolen on your behalf, and burned the villages of your enemies in the north." Horrified, the king says: "But I have no enemies in the north!" "Well," says the knight, "you do now."

A truly great queen was old Lizzie,
She went rushing around being busy.
Many men were besotted,
But her teeth had all rotted,
And her hair was all wild, red, and frizzy.

Why are medieval peasants always rebelling?
Because resistance is feudal.

How did the policeman know where to look for the body of Richard III?
He had a hunch.

How did Henry VIII get from battle to battle?
By chopper.

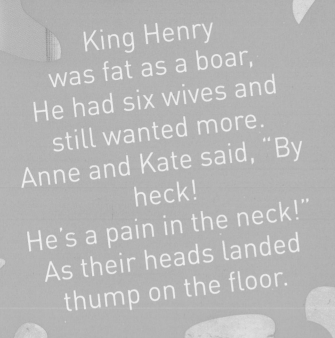

King Henry
was fat as a boar,
He had six wives and
still wanted more.
Anne and Kate said, "By
heck!
He's a pain in the neck!"
As their heads landed
thump on the floor.

Which knight loved to throw
unexpected birthday parties?
Sir Pryze!

Who is the biggest chicken-
killer in Shakespeare?
Macbeth, because he
committed murder
most fowl.

Did you hear about the mad scientist who invented a gas that could burn through anything? Now he's trying to invent something to hold it in!

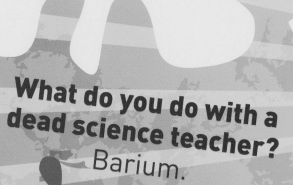

What do you do with a dead science teacher?
Barium.

What do you call it when you get struck by lightning?
A shocking experience.

Why did the science teacher tell the student he should become a weather reporter?
Because he was an expert on wind.

100

Mouse 1: I've trained that crazy scientist at last!
Mouse 2: How have you done that?
Mouse 1: I'm not sure, but every time I run through the maze and ring the bell, he gives me a lump of cheese.

How do you tell the difference between the sciences?

If it stinks, it's chemistry; if it's green or wriggly, it's biology; and if it doesn't work, it's physics.

What were the scientist's last words? Now for the taste test.

Did you hear about the mad scientist who put dynamite in his refrigerator?

They say he blew his cool.

How many drops of acid does it take to make a stink bomb?
Quite a phew.

What sort of ghosts haunt chemistry labs?
Methylated spirits.

How do you make anti-freeze?
Steal her pyjamas.

How can you tell that your chemistry teacher has died?
He fails to react.

Susan: My science teacher reminds me of the sea.
Dad: Really, dear. Do you mean she's deep and calm, but sometimes stormy?
Susan: No, she makes me sick!

What sign did the science teacher hang on the lab door?
Gone nuclear fission.

If a lightning bolt hits the back of a train, how long will it take to reach the driver?
It depends on whether he's a good conductor.

What's the most important thing to remember in chemistry?
Don't lick the spoon.

My teacher threw sodium chloride at me.
That's a salt!

Two atoms bumped into each other.
First atom: Oh dear, I think I've lost a neutron!
Second atom: Are you sure?
First atom: I'm positive!

What's special about irradiated cats?
They have 18 half-lives.

What did one lightning bolt say to the other lightning bolt?
You're shocking.

What do you call robot poo?
R2 doo doo.

104

A mosquito was heard
to complain
That a chemist had
poisoned his brain.
The cause of his sorrow
Was paradichloro-
diphenyltrichloroethane.

Why did the
chemist cut off
one of her legs?
To reduce her
carbon footprint.

Teacher:
Can you tell
me what HNO$_3$ is?
Student: Um . . . It's on
the tip of my tongue, sir.
Teacher: Well, you'd
better spit it out, it's
nitric acid!

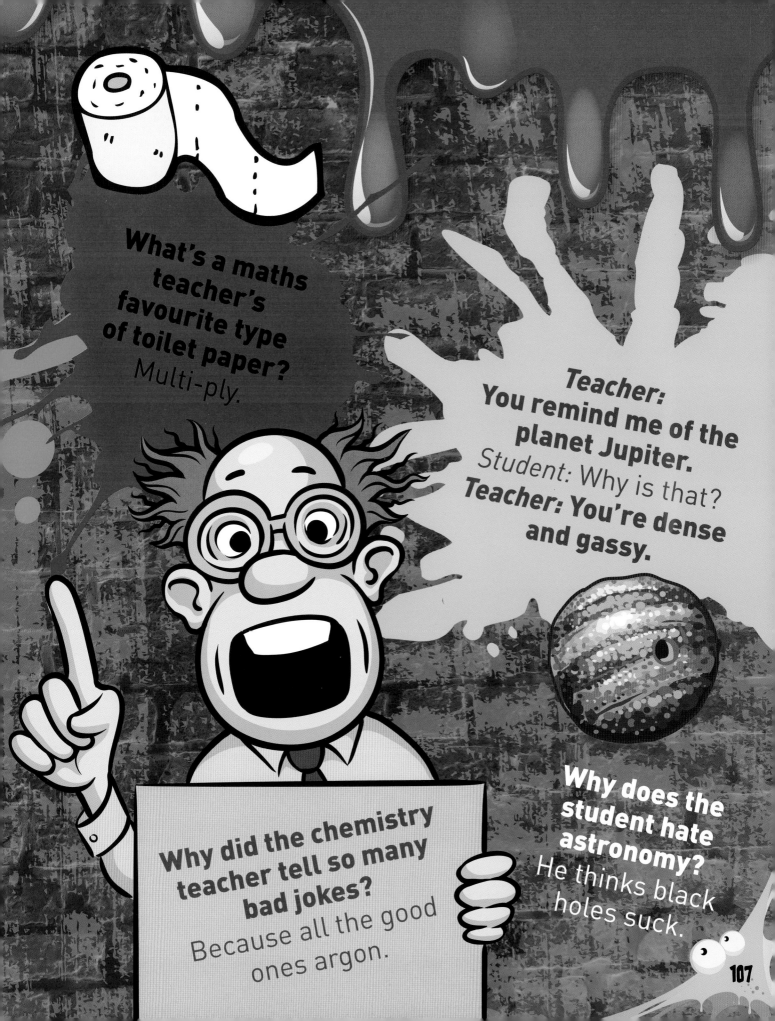

What's a maths teacher's favourite type of toilet paper?
Multi-ply.

Teacher: You remind me of the planet Jupiter.
Student: Why is that?
Teacher: You're dense and gassy.

Why did the chemistry teacher tell so many bad jokes?
Because all the good ones argon.

Why does the student hate astronomy?
He thinks black holes suck.

Why did Pete change his name to Coal? He was under pressure.

Where does illegal light end up? In a prism.

A priest, a lawyer, and an engineer are to be guillotined. The priest puts his head on the block, the rope is pulled, and nothing happens. He declares he's been saved by divine intervention and is released. The lawyer puts his head on the block, and again, the rope doesn't release the blade. He claims he can't be executed twice for the same crime and is set free. The engineer places his head under the guillotine. He looks up at the release mechanism and says: "Wait a minute, I see your problem . . ."

What is a computer virus?
A terminal illness.

Doctor: I have some good news.
Patient: What is it?
Doctor: We are going to name a disease after you.

How do you make a tissue dance?
Put a little boogie in it.

Why did the germ cross the microscope?
To get to the other slide.

What's green and hangs off trees?
Giraffe snot.

What's a sick joke?
Something that comes up in conversation.

Surgeon: I'm afraid we have to operate on you again. You see, I left my rubber gloves inside you.
Patient: I don't mind paying for them, if you'll just leave me alone.

Scientists say that 90% of all dollar bills carry germs.
Not true! Even a germ can't live on a buck these days.

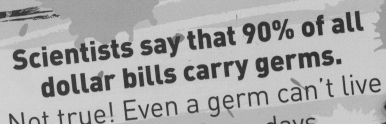

Why did the cookie go to the hospital?
Because he felt crumby.

Why did the computer keep sneezing?
It had a virus.

Have you seen the movie *Constipated*?
No, it hasn't come out yet.

Patient: Doctor, I think I'm a bridge!
Doctor: What's come over you?
Patient: Two cars, a truck and a bus.

Where do you bury lopsided people?
A-symmetry.

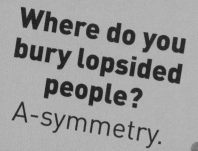

How do crazy people go through the forest?
They take the psycho path.

Patient: Doctor, you've taken out my tonsils, my adenoids, my gallbladder, my varicose veins, and my appendix, but I still don't feel well.
Doctor: That's quite enough out of you!

A little brown paper bag goes to the doctor and says, "I'm not well." The doctor tears a bit off him for tests. One week later, the bag goes back for the results. "I'm afraid you've got an inherited illness," the doctor tells him. The bag says, "How could I? I'm only a little bag." The doctor says, "Your mum or dad must have been a carrier."

What's grey with red spots? An elephant with measles.

Doctor: I have some bad news and some very bad news. Patient: Well, give me the bad news first. **Doctor: The lab called with your test results. They said you have 24 hours to live.** Patient: 24 hours! That's terrible! What's the very bad news? **Doctor: I've been trying to reach you since yesterday.**

Sister: What are you giving Dad for his birthday? Brother: Last year I gave him chickenpox. This year, I might just give him a cold.

114

A chemist finds a man leaning against the wall of his pharmacy. "What's wrong with him?" says the chemist. His assistant replies, "He came in for cough syrup, but I couldn't find any, so I gave him laxatives." "Idiot!" says the chemist. "You can't treat a cough with laxatives." "Of course you can," the assistant replies. "Look at him now, he's too afraid to cough!"

Patient: Doctor, you know those pills you gave me for my stomach?
Doctor: What about them?
Patient: They keep rolling off in the middle of the night!

Why did doctors abandon the custom of bloodletting? Because it was all in vein.

Why was the organ donor so tired after the operation?
He had really put his heart into it.

Deafness is becoming quite a problem for me. I never thought I'd hear myself say that.

Why should you never argue with your doctor?
Because he has inside information.

Why should you never lie to an X-ray technician?
Because he can see right through you.

Why did the woman avoid funerals?
She was not a mourning person.

What happens to people if their noses and feet are built backwards?
Their feet smell and their noses run.

What happened to the man who swallowed a £10 note?
No change yet.

What do you call ten years without a toothbrush?
Terrible tooth decade.

Did you hear about the man who had to have his left side amputated?
He's all right now.

117

A man was recovering in the hospital after a serious accident. He shouted, "Doctor, doctor, I can't feel my legs!" The doctor replied, "I know, I've cut off your hands."

Doctor: That's a terrible cough you've got.
Patient: Consumption be done about it?

The medical student had to learn what the measles were. He did it from scratch.

Without correct instruments, the surgeon had to operate using plumber's tools. It was a gut-wrenching experience.

If you say you have bad skin, I'd say that was a pore excuse.

Why should you be kind to your dentist? Because he has fillings, too.

Nurses who look after patients with spots do a great job. But sometimes they get paid a measley salary.

What happened to the skeleton that sat by the fire all night?
He was bone dry.

Why are fried onions like a photocopier?
They keep repeating themselves.

Why didn't the skeleton jump off the cliff?
Because he didn't have the guts.

Why did Frankenstein's monster have a stiff arm?
He had run out of elbow grease.

Why did the skeleton stay out in the snow all night?
He was a numbskull.

I don't think I should have eaten that burrito!
Why do you say that?
It's just a gut feeling.

What do you get when you cross a skunk with Frankenstein's monster?
Stinkenstein.

How do you make a skeleton laugh?
Tickle his funny bone.

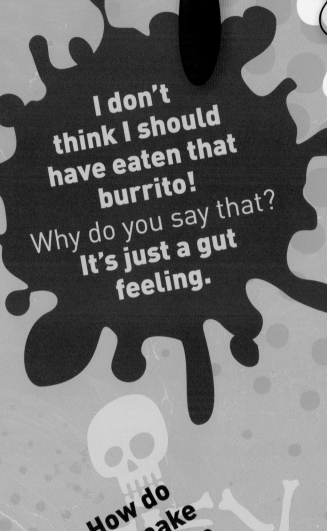

121

If you're American when you're outside the bathroom what are you when you are inside?
Eur-o-pean.

What's the funniest bone in the body?
The humerus.

I have to go to the doctor's, my neck's gone floppy!
Chin up!

I made a pot of fish eye soup.
It should see me through the week.

Professor: Today I will be talking about the liver and the spleen.
Student: Oh no, if there's one thing I can't stand, it's an organ recital!

What does Frankenstein's monster call a screwdriver? Dad.

Which human organ never dies? The liver!

What do you get if you cross a mouse and a deer? Mickey Moose.

Dentist: I have to pull out your bad tooth, but don't worry it will take just five minutes.
Patient: And how much will it cost?
Dentist: £90.00.
Patient: £90.00 for just a few minutes work???
Dentist: I can extract it very slowly if you like.

What do you get when you cross a potato with a sponge?
I don't know, but it sure holds a lot of gravy!

I crossed a phone with a skunk
And now the service stinks.

What did the man say when he found someone blocking his path to the toilet?
Urine my way.

Why are frogs so happy?
Because they can eat whatever bugs them.

What do you do when two snails have a fight?
Leave them to slug it out!

Where do bees go to the toilet?
At the BP station.

How can you tell which end of a worm is which?
Tickle it in the middle and see which end laughs.

There was an old woman from Ryde
Who ate too many apples and died.
The apples fermented
Inside the lamented
And made cider inside her inside.

England doesn't have a kidney bank. But it does have a Liverpool.

Two silkworms had a race. They ended up in a tie.

I don't think I want a spine. It's holding me back.

1st scientist: Did you know that I'm thinking of cloning myself? 2nd scientist: Now wouldn't that be just like you!

I once thought about cloning a new, more efficient brain. But then I realized I was getting a head of myself.

Why do French people love eating snails? Because they don't like fast food.

Why are skeletons usually so calm? Nothing gets under their skin.

Why did the guests at the cannibal's party run away? They heard he would be serving finger foods.